To W.J.Hare,
with Love,
        J.F.H. 23.3.81.

CHURCH
POEMS

STANTON LOW, BUCKS

CHURCH POEMS

JOHN BETJEMAN

ILLUSTRATED BY
JOHN PIPER

JOHN MURRAY

© John Betjeman 1932, 1937, 1940, 1945,
1948, 1954, 1966, 1974, 1981

In addition to new poems, this volume includes several
that appeared in *Poems in the Porch* (S.P.C.K.)
but have long been out of print.

First published 1981
by John Murray (Publishers) Ltd
50 Albemarle Street, London w1x 4bd

Printed in Great Britain by
W & J Mackay Ltd, Chatham

British Library Cataloguing in Publication Data
Betjeman, *Sir* John
Church poems.
I. Title
821′.9′12   PR6025.A858A17
0–7195–3784–3 *trade edition*
0–7195–3797–5 *limited edition*

Contents

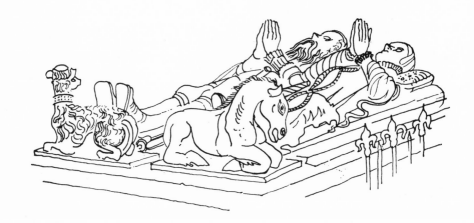

Preface

Churches are preserved so long as people like them, even if they don't like them much. My friend, the Rev. Harry Williams, erstwhile Dean of Trinity College, Cambridge and a famous theologian, says that churches are banks of affection, and it is affection that keeps them standing. When Mr Piper and I were doing the Shell Guides, we looked in at every church, that is to say every parish church, for we are both Church of England. Along with the building went the Vicar, the Verger and the Parish Magazine, and so our affection for churches grew.

From church to church they hurried us, did the Shell Guides, and on our journeys I made up verses, some of which are reprinted here. Mr Piper drew the sketches, which indicate atmosphere as well as architecture and its date. Both of us were none too solemn, and we were much helped by the photography of the late Edwin Smith, who could find a significant detail in a church—an oil lamp, a bell rope, or a harmonium which would conjure up a whole parish of people.

I hope this book will humanise churches a bit for those who think of them only in terms of architectural style or rateable value. Without a church I think a place lacks its heart and identity.

JOHN BETJEMAN

A Lincolnshire Tale

Kirkby with Muckby-cum-Sparrowby-cum-Spinx
Is down a long lane in the county of Lincs,
And often on Wednesdays, well-harnessed and spruce,
I would drive into Wiss over Winderby Sluice.

A whacking great sunset bathed level and drain
From Kirkby with Muckby to Beckby-on-Bain,
And I saw, as I journeyed, my marketing done
Old Caistorby tower take the last of the sun.

The night air grew nippy. An autumn mist roll'd
(In a scent of dead cabbages) down from the wold,
In the ocean of silence that flooded me round
The crunch of the wheels was a comforting sound.

The lane lengthened narrowly into the night
With the Bain on its left bank, the drain on its right,
And feebly the carriage-lamps glimmered ahead
When all of a sudden *the pony fell dead.*

The remoteness was awful, the stillness intense,
Of invisible fenland, around and immense;
And out of the dark, with a roar and a swell,
Swung, hollowly thundering, Speckleby bell.

Though my self the Archdeacon for many a year,
I had not summoned courage for visiting here;
Our incumbents were mostly eccentric or sad
But—*the Speckleby Rector was said to be mad.*

Oh cold was the ev'ning and tall was the tower
And strangely compelling the tenor bell's power!
As loud on the reed-beds and strong through the dark
It toll'd from the church in the tenantless park.

The mansion was ruined, the empty demesne
Was slowly reverting to marshland again—
Marsh where the village was, grass in the Hall,
And the church and the Rectory waiting to fall.

And even in springtime with kingcups about
And stumps of old oak-trees attempting to sprout,
'Twas a sinister place, neither fenland nor wold,
And doubly forbidding in darkness and cold.

As down swung the tenor, a beacon of sound,
Over listening acres of waterlogged ground
I stood by the tombs to see pass and repass
The gleam of a taper, through clear leaded glass,

And such lighting of lights in the thunderous roar
That heart summoned courage to hand at the door;
I grated it open on scents I knew well,
The dry smell of damp rot, the hassocky smell.

What a forest of woodwork in ochres and grains
Unevenly doubled in diamonded panes,
And over the plaster, so textured with time,
Sweet discoloration of umber and lime.

The candles ensconced on each high pannelled pew
Brought the caverns of brass-studded baize into view,
But the roof and its rafters were lost to the sight
As they soared to the dark of the Lincolnshire night:

And high from the chancel arch paused to look down
A sign-painter's beasts in their fight for the Crown,
While massive, impressive, and still as the grave
A three-decker pulpit frowned over the nave.

Shall I ever forget what a stillness was there
When the bell ceased its tolling and thinned on the air?
Then an opening door showed a long pair of hands
And the Rector himself in his gown and his bands.

*   *   *   *   *

Such a fell Visitation I shall not forget,
Such a rush through the dark, that I rush through it yet,
And I pray, as the bells ring o'er fenland and hill,
That the Speckleby acres be tenantless still.

Westgate-on-Sea

Hark, I hear the bells of Westgate,
   I will tell you what they sigh,
Where those minarets and steeples
   Prick the open Thanet sky.

Happy bells of eighteen-ninety,
   Bursting from your freestone tower!
Recalling laurel, shrubs and privet,
   Red geraniums in flower.

Feet that scamper on the asphalt
   Through the Borough Council grass,
Till they hide inside the shelter
   Bright with ironwork and glass,

Striving chains of ordered children
   Purple by the sea-breeze made,
Striving on to prunes and suet
   Past the shops on the Parade.

Some with wire around their glasses,
   Some with wire across their teeth,
Writhing frames for running noses
   And the drooping lip beneath.

Church of England bells of Westgate!
   On this balcony I stand,
White the woodwork wriggles round me,
   Clock towers rise on either hand.

For me in my timber arbour
You have one more message yet,
"Plimsolls, plimsolls in the summer,
Oh goloshes in the wet!"

Verses turned
in aid of A Public Subscription (1952)
towards the restoration of the
Church of St. Katherine
Chiselhampton, Oxon

Across the wet November night
The church is bright with candlelight
And waiting Evensong.
A single bell with plaintive strokes
Pleads louder than the stirring oaks
The leafless lanes along.

It calls the choirboys from their tea
And villagers, the two or three,
Damp down the kitchen fire,
Let out the cat, and up the lane
Go paddling through the gentle rain
Of misty Oxfordshire.

CHISELHAMPTON, OXON

How warm the many candles shine
On SAMUEL DOWBIGGIN's design
   For this interior neat,
These high box pews of Georgian days
Which screen us from the public gaze
   When we make answer meet;

How gracefully their shadow falls
On bold pilasters down the walls
   And on the pulpit high.
The chandeliers would twinkle gold
As pre-Tractarian sermons roll'd
   Doctrinal, sound and dry.

14

From that west gallery no doubt
The viol and serpent tooted out
   The Tallis tune to Ken,
And firmly at the end of prayers
The clerk below the pulpit stairs
   Would thunder out "Amen."

But every wand'ring thought will cease
Before the noble altarpiece
   With carven swags array'd,
For there in letters all may read
The Lord's Commandments, Prayer and Creed.
   Are decently display'd.

On country mornings sharp and clear
The penitent in faith draw near
   And kneeling here below
Partake the Heavenly Banquet spread
Of Sacramental Wine and Bread
   And JESUS' presence know.

And must that plaintive bell in vain
Plead loud along the dripping lane?
   And must the building fall?
Not while we love the Church and live
And of our charity will give
   Our much, our more, our all.

Bristol and Clifton

"Yes I was only sidesman here when last
You came to Evening Communion.
But now I have retired from the bank
I have more leisure time for church finance.
We moved into a somewhat larger house
Than when you knew us in Manilla Road.
This is the window to my lady wife.
You cannot see it now, but in the day
The greens and golds are truly wonderful."

"How very sad. I do not mean about
The window, but I mean about the death
Of Mrs. Battlecock. When did she die?"

"Two years ago when we had just moved in
To Pembroke Road. I rather fear the stairs
And basement kitchen were too much for her—
Not that, of course, she did the servants' work—
But supervising servants all the day
Meant quite a lot of climbing up and down."
"How very sad. Poor Mrs. Battlecock."
" 'The glory that men do lives after them,'[1]
And so I gave this window in her name.
It's executed by a Bristol firm;
The lady artist who designed it, made
The figure of the lady on the left
Something like Mrs. Battlecock."
"How nice."

[1] Shakespeare, of course.

"Yes, was it not? We had
A stained glass window on the stairs at home,
In Pembroke Road. But not so good as this.
This window is the glory of the church
At least I think so—and the unstained oak
Looks very chaste beneath it. When I gave
The oak, that brass inscription on your right
Commemorates the fact, the Dorcas Club
Made these blue kneelers, though we do not kneel:
We leave that to the Roman Catholics."
"How very nice, indeed. How very nice."

"Seeing I have some knowledge of finance
Our kind Parochial Church Council made
Me People's Warden, and I'm glad to say
That our collections are still keeping up.
The chancel has been flood-lit, and the stove
Which used to heat the church was obsolete.
So now we've had some radiators fixed
Along the walls and eastward of the aisles;
This last I thought of lest at any time
A Ritualist should be inducted here
And want to put up altars. He would find
The radiators inconvenient.
Our only ritual here is with the Plate;
I think we make it dignified enough.
I take it up myself, and afterwards,
Count the Collection on the vestry safe."

"Forgive me, aren't we talking rather loud?
I think I see a woman praying there."

"Praying? The service is all over now
And here's the verger waiting to turn out
The lights and lock the church up. She cannot
Be Loyal Church of England. Well, good-bye.
Time flies. I must be going. Come again.
There are some pleasant people living here.
I know the Inskips very well indeed."

Calvinistic Evensong

The six bells stopped, and in the dark I heard
Cold silence wait the Calvinistic word;
For Calvin now the soft oil lamps are lit
Hands on their hymnals six old women sit.
Black gowned and sinister he now appears,
Curate-in-charge of aged parish fears.
Let, unaccompanied, that psalm begin
Which deals most harshly with the fruits of sin!
Boy! pump the organ! let the anthem flow
With promise for the chosen saints below!
Pregnant with warning the globed elm trees wait
Fresh coffin-wood beside the churchyard gate.
And that mauve hat three cherries decorate
Next week shall topple from its trembling perch
While wet fields reek like some long empty church.

St. Barnabas, Oxford

How long was the peril, how breathless the day,
In topaz and beryl, the sun dies away,
His rays lying static at quarter to six
On polychromatical lacing of bricks.
Good Lord, as the angelus floats down the road
Byzantine St. Barnabas, be Thine Abode.

Where once the fritillaries hung in the grass
A baldachin pillar is guarding the Mass.
Farewell to blue meadows we loved not enough,
And elms in whose shadows were Glanville and Clough
Not poets but clergymen hastened to meet
Thy redden'd remorselessness, Cardigan Street.

19

Undenominational

Undenominational
  But still the church of God
He stood in his conventicle
  And ruled it with a rod.

Undenominational
  The walls around him rose,
The lamps within their brackets shook
  To hear the hymns he chose.

"Glory" "Gopsel" "Russell Place"
  "Wrestling Jacob" "Rock"
"Saffron Walden" "Safe at Home"
  "Dorking" "Plymouth Dock"

I slipped about the chalky lane
  That runs without the park,
I saw the lone conventicle
  A beacon in the dark.

Revival ran along the hedge
  And made my spirit whole
When steam was on the window panes
  And glory in my soul.

Holy Trinity, Sloane Street
MCMVII

An Acolyte singeth
Light six white tapers with the Flame of Art,
Send incense wreathing to the lily flowers,
And, with your cool hands white,
Swing the warm censer round my bruised heart,
Drop, dove-grey eyes, your penitential showers
On this pale acolyte.

A confirmandus continueth
The tall red house soars upward to the stars,
The doors are chased with sardonyx and gold,
And in the long white room
Thin drapery draws backward to unfold
Cadogan Square between the window-bars
And Whistler's mother knitting in the gloom.

The Priest endeth
How many hearts turn Motherward to-day?
(Red roses faint not on your twining stems!)
Bronze triptych doors unswing!
Wait, restive heart, wait, rounded lips, to pray,
Mid beaten copper interset with gems
Behold! Behold! your King!

Hymn

The Church's Restoration
　　In eighteen-eighty-three
Has left for contemplation
　　Not what there used to be.
How well the ancient woodwork
　　Looks round the Rect'ry hall,
Memorial of the good work
　　Of him who plann'd it all.

He who took down the pew-ends
　　And sold them anywhere
But kindly spared a few ends
　　Work'd up into a chair.
O worthy persecution
　　Of dust! O hue divine!
O cheerful substitution,
　　Thou varnishéd pitch-pine!

Church furnishing! Church furnishing!
　　Sing art and crafty praise!
He gave the brass for burnishing
　　He gave the thick red baize,
He gave the new addition,
　　Pull'd down the dull old aisle,
—To pave the sweet transition
　　He gave th' encaustic tile.

Of marble brown and veinéd
　　He did the pulpit make;

He order'd windows stainéd
   Light red and crimson lake.
Sing on, with hymns uproarious,
   Ye humble and aloof,
Look up! and oh how glorious
   He has restored the roof!

Uffington

Tonight we feel the muffled peal
   Hang on the village like a pall;
It overwhelms the towering elms—
   That death-reminding dying fall;
The very sky no longer high
   Comes down within the reach of all.
Imprisoned in a cage of sound
Even the trivial seems profound.

St. Bartholomew's Hospital

The ghost of Rahere still walks in Bart's;
It gives an impulse to generous hearts,
It looks on pain with a pitying eye,
It teaches us never to fear to die.

Eight hundred years of compassion and care
Have hallowed its fountain, stones and Square.
Pray for us all as we near the gate—
St. Bart the Less and St. Bart the Great.

Sunday Afternoon Service in St. Enodoc Church, Cornwall

Come on! come on! This hillock hides the spire,
Now that one and now none. As winds about
The burnished path through lady's finger, thyme
And bright varieties of saxifrage,
So grows the tinny tenor faint or loud
And all things draw towards St. Enodoc.

Come on! come on! and it is five to three.

Paths, unfamiliar to golfers' brogues,
Cross the eleventh fairway broadside on
And leave the fourteenth tee for thirteenth green,
Ignoring Royal and Ancient, bound for God.
  Come on! come on! no longer bare of foot,
The sole grows hot in London shoes again.
Jack Lambourne in his Sunday navy-blue
Wears tie and collar, all from Selfridge's.
There's Enid with a silly parasol,
And Graham in gray flannel with a crease
Across the middle of his coat which lay
Pressed 'neath the box of his Meccano set,
Sunday to Sunday.
              Still Come on! come on!
The tinny tenor. Hover-flies remain
More than a moment on a ragwort bunch,
And people's passing shadows don't disturb
Red Admirals basking with their wings apart.
  A mile of sunny, empty sand away,
A mile of shallow pools and lugworm casts,

Safe, faint and surfy, laps the lowest tide.
　　Even the villas have a Sunday look.
The Ransome mower's locked into the shed.
"I have a splitting headache from the sun,"
And bedroom windows flutter cheerful chintz
Where, double-aspirined, a mother sleeps;
While father in the loggia reads a book,
Large, desultory, birthday-present size,
Published with coloured plates by *Country Life*,
A Bernard Darwin on *The English Links*
Or Braid and Taylor on *The Mashie Shot*.
Come on! come on! he thinks of Monday's round—
Come on! come on! that interlocking grip!
Come on! come on! he drops into a doze—
Come on! come on! more far and far away
The children climb a final stile to church;
Electoral Roll still flapping in the porch—
Then the cool silence of St. Enodoc.

My eyes, recovering in the sudden shade,
Discern the long-known little things within—
A map of France in damp above my pew,
Grey-blue of granite in the small arcade
(Late Perp: and not a Parker specimen
But roughly hewn on windy Bodmin Moor),
The modest windows palely glazed with green,
The smooth slate floor, the rounded wooden roof,
The Norman arch, the cable-moulded font—
All have a humble and West Country look.
Oh "drastic restoration" of the guide!
Oh three-light window by a Plymouth firm!
Absurd, truncated screen! oh sticky pews!

Embroidered altar-cloth! untended lamps!
So soaked in worship you are loved too well
For that dispassionate and critic stare
That I would use beyond the parish bounds
Biking in high-banked lanes from tower to tower
On sunny, antiquarian afternoons.
    Come on! come on! a final pull. Tom Blake
Stalks over from the bell-rope to his pew
Just as he slopes about the windy cliffs
Looking for wreckage in a likely tide,
Nor gives the Holy Table glance or nod.
A rattle as red baize is drawn aside,
Miss Rhoda Poulden pulls the tremolo,
The oboe, flute and vox humana stops;
A Village Voluntary fills the air
And ceases suddenly as it began,
Save for one oboe faintly humming on,
As slow the weary clergyman subsides
Tired with his bike-ride from the parish church.
He runs his hands once, twice, across his face
"Dearly beloved . . ." and a bumble-bee
Zooms itself free into the churchyard sun
And so my thoughts this happy Sabbathtide.
    Where deep cliffs loom enormous, where cascade
Mesembryanthemum and stone-crop down,
Where the gull looks no larger than a lark
Hung midway twixt the cliff-top and the sand,
Sun-shadowed valleys roll along the sea.
Forced by the backwash, see the nearest wave
Rise to a wall of huge translucent green
And crumble into spray along the top

Blown seaward by the land-breeze. Now she breaks
And in an arch of thunder plunges down
To burst and tumble, foam on top of foam,
Criss-crossing, baffled, sucked and shot again,
A waterfall of whiteness, down a rock,
Without a source but roller's furthest reach:
And tufts of sea-pink, high and dry for years,
Are flooded out of ledges, boulders seem
No bigger than a pebble washed about
In this tremendous tide. Oh kindly slate!
To give me shelter in this crevice dry.
These shivering stalks of bent-grass, lucky plant,
Have better chance than I to last the storm.
Oh kindly slate of these unaltered cliffs,
Firm, barren substrate of our windy fields!
Oh lichened slate in walls, they knew your worth
Who raised you up to make this House of God
What faith was his, that dim, that Cornish saint,
Small rushlight of a long-forgotten church,
Who lived with God on this unfriendly shore,
Who knew He made the Atlantic and the stones
And destined seamen here to end their lives
Dashed on a rock, rolled over in the surf,
And not one hair forgotten. Now they lie
In centuries of sand beside the church.
Less pitiable are they than the corpse
Of a large golfer, only four weeks dead,
This sunlit and sea-distant afternoon.
"Praise ye the Lord!" and in another key
The Lord's name by harmonium be praised.
"The Second Evening and the Fourteenth Psalm."

Church of England thoughts
occasioned by hearing the bells
of Magdalen Tower
from the Botanic Garden, Oxford
on St. Mary Magdalen's Day

I see the urn against the yew,
    The sunlit urn of sculptured stone,
I see its shapely shadow fall
On this enormous garden wall
    Which makes a kingdom of its own.

A grassy kingdom sweet to view
    With tiger lilies still in flower
And beds of umbelliferæ
Ranged in Linnaean symmetry,
    All in the sound of Magdalen tower.

A multiplicity of bells,
    A changing cadence, rich and deep
Swung from those pinnacles on high
To fill the trees and flood the sky
    And rock the sailing clouds to sleep.

A Church of England sound, it tells
    Of "moderate" worship, God and State,
Where matins congregations go
Conservative and good and slow
    To elevations of the plate.

And loud through resin-scented chines
　　And purple rhododendrons roll'd,
I hear the bells for Eucharist
From churches blue with incense mist
　　Where reredoses twinkle gold.

Chapels-of-ease by railway lines
　　And humble streets and smells of gas
I hear your plaintive ting-tangs call
From many a gabled western wall
　　To Morning Prayer or Holy Mass.

In country churches old and pale
　　I hear the changes smoothly rung
And watch the coloured sallies fly
From rugged hands to rafters high
　　As round and back the bells are swung.

Before the spell begins to fail,
　　Before the bells have lost their power,
Before the grassy kingdom fade
And Oxford traffic roar invade,
　　I thank the bells of Magdalen Tower.

Lines on the New Buildings, Magdalen College, Oxford

composed by The Reverend James Hurdis D.D. (1763–1801)
Sometime Fellow and Professor of Poetry at Oxford
and added to by John Betjeman in 1980

How gracefully it rests upon its shadow
In the deep quiet of this walled-in meadow,
Grave, grey and classical and on its own
A hymn by Addison in Oxford stone
Magdalen New Buildings! Glad was I when young
To hear, in your wide arch, the quarters rung
When I was twelve, as deep they were to me
As now they sound when I am seventy three.
Let me go on in Hurdis's blank verse
So very blank and to the point and terse;
He was a Fellow once and in his time
Deeply loved Magdalen and avoided rhyme.
"It is enough for me to hear the sound
Of the remote exhilarating peal
Now dying all away, now faintly heard,
And now with loud and musical relapse
Its mellow changes huddling on the ear.
So have I stood at eve on Isis banks,
To hear the merry Christchurch bells rejoice,
So have I sat too in thy honoured shades
Distinguished Magdalen on Cherwell's bank
To hear thy silver Wolsey tones so sweet.
And so too have I paused and held my oar
And suffered the slow stream to bear me home,
While Wykeham's peal along the meadow ran."

Sunday Morning, King's Cambridge

File into yellow candle light, fair choristers of King's
    Lost in the shadowy silence of canopied Renaissance stalls
In blazing glass above the dark glow skies and thrones and wings
    Blue, ruby, gold and green between the whiteness of the walls
And with what rich precision the stonework soars and springs
    To fountain out a spreading vault—a shower that never falls.

The white of windy Cambridge courts, the cobbles brown and dry,
    The gold of plaster Gothic with ivy overgrown,
The apple-red, the silver fronts, the wide green flats and high,
    The yellowing elm-trees circled out on islands of their own—
Oh, here behold all colours change that catch the flying sky
    To waves of pearly light that heave along the shafted stone.

In far East Anglian churches, the clasped hands lying long
    Recumbent on sepulchral slabs or effigied in brass
Buttress with prayer this vaulted roof so white and light and strong
    And countless congregations as the generation pass
Join choir and great crowned organ case, in centuries of song
    To praise Eternity contained in Time and coloured glass.

A Lincolnshire Church

Greyly tremendous the thunder
Hung over the width of the wold
But here the green marsh was alight
In a huge cloud cavern of gold,
And there, on a gentle eminence,
Topping some ash trees, a tower

35

Silver and brown in the sunlight,
Worn by sea-wind and shower,
Lincolnshire Middle Pointed.
And around it, turning their backs,
The usual sprinkle of villas;
The usual woman in slacks,
Cigarette in her mouth,
Regretting Americans, stands
As a wireless croons in the kitchen
Manicuring her hands.
Dear old, bloody old England
Of telegraph poles and tin,
Seemingly so indifferent
And with so little soul to win.
What sort of church, I wonder?
The path is a grassy mat,
And grass is drowning the headstones
Sloping this way and that.
"Cathedral Glass" in the windows,
A roof of unsuitable slate—
Restored with a vengeance, for certain,
About eighteen-eighty-eight.
The door swung easily open
(Unlocked, for these parts, is odd)
And there on the South aisle altar
Is the tabernacle of God.
There where the white light flickers
By the white and silver veil,
A wafer dipped in a wine-drop
Is the Presence the angels hail,
Is God who created the Heavens

And the wide green marsh as well
Who sings in the sky with the skylark
Who calls in the evening bell,
Is God who prepared His coming
With fruit of the earth for his food
With stone for building His churches
And trees for making His rood.
There where the white light flickers,
Our Creator is with us yet,
To be worshipped by you and the woman
Of the slacks and the cigarette.

* * * * *

The great door shuts, and lessens
That roar of churchyard trees
And the Presence of God Incarnate
Has brought me to my knees.
"I acknowledge my transgressions"
The well-known phrases rolled
With thunder sailing over
From the heavily clouded wold.
"And my sin is ever before me."
There in the lighted East
He stood in that lowering sunlight,
An Indian Christian priest.
And why he was here in Lincolnshire
I neither asked nor knew,
Nor whether his flock was many
Nor whether his flock was few
I thought of the heaving waters
That bore him from sun glare harsh

Of some Indian Anglican Mission
To this green enormous marsh.
There where the white light flickers,
Here, as the rains descend,
The same mysterious Godhead
Is welcoming His friend.

On Hearing the Full Peal of Ten Bells from Christ Church, Swindon, Wilts.

Your peal of ten ring over then this town,
Ring on my men nor ever ring them down.
This winter chill, let sunset spill cold fire
On villa'd hill and on Sir Gilbert's spire,
So new, so high, so pure, so broach'd, so tall.
Long run the thunder of the bells through all!

Oh still white headstones on these fields of sound
Hear you the wedding joybells wheeling round?
Oh brick-built breeding boxes of new souls,
Hear how the pealing through the louvres rolls!
Now birth and death-reminding bells ring clear,
Loud under 'planes and over changing gear.

Christmas

The bells of waiting Advent ring,
   The Tortoise stove is lit again
And lamp-oil light across the night
   Has caught the streaks of winter rain
In many a stained-glass window sheen
From Crimson Lake to Hooker's Green.

The holly in the windy hedge
   And round the Manor House the yew
Will soon be stripped to deck the ledge,
   The altar, font and arch and pew,
So that the villagers can say
"The church looks nice" on Christmas Day.

Provincial public houses blaze
   And Corporation tramcars clang,
On lighted tenements I gaze
   Where paper decorations hang,
And bunting in the red Town Hall
Says "Merry Christmas to you all."

And London shops on Christmas Eve
   Are strung with silver bells and flowers
As hurrying clerks the City leave
   To pigeon-haunted classic towers,
And marbled clouds go scudding by
The many-steepled London sky.

And girls in slacks remember Dad,

And oafish louts remember Mum,
And sleepless children's hearts are glad,
And Christmas-morning bells say "Come!"
Even to shining ones who dwell
Safe in the Dorchester Hotel.

And is it true? And is it true,
This most tremendous tale of all,
Seen in a stained-glass window's hue,
A Baby in an ox's stall?
The Maker of the stars and sea
Become a Child on earth for me?

And is it true? For if it is,
No loving fingers tying strings
Around those tissued fripperies,
The sweet and silly Christmas things,
Bath salts and inexpensive scent
And hideous tie so kindly meant,

No love that in a family dwells,
No carolling in frosty air,
Nor all the steeple-shaking bells
Can with this single Truth compare—
That God was Man in Palestine
And lives to-day in Bread and Wine.

St. Saviour's, Aberdeen Park, Highbury, London, N.

With oh such peculiar branching and over-reaching of wire
    Trolley-bus standards pick their threads from the London sky
Diminishing up the perspective, Highbury-bound retire
    Threads and buses and standards with plane trees volleying by
And, more peculiar still, that ever-increasing spire
    Bulges over the housetops, polychromatic and high.

Stop the trolley-bus, stop! And here, where the roads unite
    Of weariest worn-out London—no cigarettes, no beer,
No repairs undertaken, nothing in stock—alight;
    For over the waste of willow-herb, look at her, sailing clear,
A great Victorian church, tall, unbroken and bright
    In a sun that's setting in Willesden and saturating us here.

These were the streets my parents knew when they loved and won—
    The brougham that crunched the gravel, the laurel-girt paths
                                     that wind,
Geranium-beds for the lawn, Venetian blinds for the sun,
    A separate tradesman's entrance, straw in the mews behind,
Just in the four-mile radius where hackney carriages run,
    Solid Italianate houses for the solid commercial mind.

These were the streets they knew; and I, by descent, belong
    To these tall neglected houses divided into flats.
Only the church remains, where carriages used to throng
    And my mother stepped out in flounces and my father
                                   stepped out in spats
To shadowy stained-glass matins or gas-lit evensong

And back in a country quiet with doffing of chimney hats.

Great red church of my parents, cruciform crossing they knew—
    Over these same encaustics they and their parents trod
Bound through a red-brick transept for a once familiar pew
    Where the organ set them singing and the sermon let them nod
And up this coloured brickwork the same long shadows grew
    As these in the stencilled chancel where I kneel in the
                                        presence of God.

Wonder beyond Time's wonders, that Bread so white and small
    Veiled in golden curtains, too mighty for men to see,
Is the Power that sends the shadows up this polychrome wall,
    Is God who created the present, the chain-smoking millions and me;
Beyond the throb of the engines is the throbbing heart of all—
    Christ, at this Highbury altar, I offer myself to Thee.

The Planster's Vision

Cut down that timber! Bells, too many and strong,
   Pouring their music through the branches bare,
   From moon-white church-towers down the windy air
Have pealed the centuries out with Evensong.
Remove those cottages, a huddled throng!
   Too many babies have been born in there,
   Too many coffins, bumping down the stair,
Carried the old their garden paths along.

I have a Vision of The Future, chum,
   The workers' flats in fields of soya beans
      Tower up like silver pencils, score on score:
And Surging Millions hear the Challenge come
   From microphones in communal canteens
      "No Right! No Wrong! All's perfect, evermore."

Diary of a Church Mouse

(Lines, written to order on a set subject,
to be spoken on the wireless.)

Here among long-discarded cassocks,
Damp stools, and half-split open hassocks,
Here where the Vicar never looks
I nibble through old service books.
Lean and alone I spend my days
Behind this Church of England baize.
I share my dark forgotten room
With two oil-lamps and half a broom.
The cleaner never bothers me,
So here I eat my frugal tea.
My bread is sawdust mixed with straw;
My jam is polish for the floor.
  Christmas and Easter may be feasts
For congregations and for priests,
And so may Whitsun. All the same,
They do not fill my meagre frame.
For me the only feast at all
Is Autumn's Harvest Festival,
When I can satisfy my want
With ears of corn around the font.
I climb the eagle's brazen head
To burrow through a loaf of bread.
I scramble up the pulpit stair
And gnaw the marrows hanging there
  It is enjoyable to taste
These items ere they go to waste,

But how annoying when one finds
That other mice with pagan minds
Come into church my food to share
Who have no proper business there.
Two field mice who have no desire
To be baptized, invade the choir.
A large and most unfriendly rat
Comes in to see what we are at.
He says he thinks there is no God
And yet he comes . . . it's rather odd.
This year he stole a sheaf of wheat
(It screened our special preacher's seat),
And prosperous mice from fields away
Come in to hear the organ play,
And under cover of its notes
Ate through the altar's sheaf of oats.
A Low Church mouse, who thinks that I
Am too papistical, and High,
Yet somehow doesn't think it wrong
To munch through Harvest Evensong,
While I, who starve the whole year through,
Must share my food with rodents who
Except at this time of the year
Not once inside the church appear.
   Within the human world I know
Such goings-on could not be so,
For human beings only do
What their religion tells them to.
They read the Bible every day
And always, night and morning, pray,
And just like me, the good church mouse,

Worship each week in God's own house,
    But all the same it's strange to me
How very full the church can be
With people I don't see at all
Except at Harvest Festival.

Wantage Bells

Now with the bells through the apple bloom
        Sunday-ly sounding
And the prayers of the nuns in their chapel gloom
        Us all surrounding,
        Where the brook flows
        Brick walls of rose
Send on the motionless meadow the bell notes rebounding.

Wall flowers are bright in their beds
        And their scent all pervading,
Withered are primroses heads
        And the hyacinth fading
        But flowers by the score
        Multitudes more
Weed flowers and seed flowers and mead flowers our paths
                                  are invading.

Where are the words to express
        Such a reckless bestowing?
The voices of birds utter less
        Than the thanks we are owing,
        Bell notes alone
        Ring praise of their own
As clear as the weed-waving brook and as evenly flowing

Autumn 1964

(FOR KAREN)

Red apples hang like globes of light
  Against this pale November haze,
And now, although the mist is white,
  In half-an-hour a day of days
Will climb into its golden height
  And Sunday bells will ring its praise.

The sparkling flint, the darkling yew,
  The red brick, less intensely red
Than hawthorn berries bright with dew
  Or leaves of creeper still unshed,
The watery sky washed clean and new,
  Are all rejoicing with the dead.

The yellowing elm shows yet some green,
  The mellowing bells exultant sound:
Never have light and colour been
  So prodigally thrown around;
And in the bells the promise tells
  Of greater light where Love is found.

On Leaving Wantage 1972

I like the way these old brick garden walls
Unevenly run down to Letcombe Brook.
I like the mist of green about the elms
In earliest leaf-time. More intensely green
The duck-weed undulates; a mud-grey trout
Hovers and darts away at my approach.

From rumpled beds on far-off new estates,
From houses over shops along the square,
From red-brick villas somewhat further out,
Ringers arrive, converging on the tower.
Third Sunday after Easter. Public ways
Reek faintly yet of last night's fish and chips.
The plumes of smoke from upright chimney-pots
Denote the death of last week's Sunday press,
While this week's waits on many a step and sill
Unopened, folded, supplements and all.

Suddenly on the unsuspecting air
The bells clash out. It seems a miracle
That leaf and flower should never even stir
In such great waves of medieval sound:
They ripple over roofs to fields and farms
So that "the fellowship of Christ's religion"
Is roused to breakfast, church or sleep again.

From this wide vale, where all our married lives
We two have lived, we now are whirled away
Momently clinging to the things we knew—
Friends, footpaths, hedges, house and animals—
Till, borne along like twigs and bits of straw,
We sink below the sliding stream of time.

Churchyards

Now when the weather starts to clear
How fresh the primrose clumps appear,
Those shining pools of springtime flower
In our churchyard. And on the tower
We see the sharp spring sunlight thrown
On all its sparkling rainwashed stone,
That tower, so built to take the light
Of sun by day and moon by night,
That centuries of weather there
Have mellowed it to twice as fair
As when it first rose new and hard
Above the sports in our churchyard.
   For churchyards then, though hallowed ground
Were not so grim as now they sound,

And horns of ale were handed round
For which churchwardens used to pay
On each especial vestry day.
'Twas thus the village drunk its beer
With its relations buried near,
And that is why we often see
Inns where the alehouse used to be
Close to the church when prayers were said
And Masses for the village dead.

   But in these latter days we've grown
To think that the memorial stone
Is quite enough for soul and clay
Until the Resurrection Day.
Perhaps it is. It's not for me
To argue on theology.

   But this I know, you're sure to find
Some headstones of the Georgian kind
In each old churchyard near and far,
Just go and see how fine they are.
Notice the lettering of that age
Spaced like a noble title-page,
The parish names cut deep and strong
To hold the shades of evening long,
The quaint and sometimes touching rhymes
By parish poets of the times,
Bellows, or reaping hook or spade
To show, perhaps, the dead man's trade,
And cherubs in the corner spaces
With wings and English ploughboy faces.

   Engraved on slate or carved in stone
These Georgian headstones hold their own.

FAWLEY, BUCKS

With craftsmanship of earlier days
Men gave in their Creator's praise.
More homely are they than the white
Italian marbles which were quite
The rage in Good King Edward's reign,
With ugly lettering, hard and plain.

    Our churches are our history shown
In wood and glass and iron and stone.
I hate to see in old churchyards
Tombstones stacked round like playing cards
Along the wall which then encloses
A trim new lawn and standard roses,
Bird-baths and objects such as fill a
Garden in some suburban villa.
The Bishop comes; the bird-bath's blessed,
Our churchyard's now "a garden of rest".
And so it may be, all the same
Graveyard's a much more honest name.

    Oh why do people waste their breath
Inventing dainty names for death?
On the old tombstones of the past
We do not read "At peace at last"
But simply "died" or plain "departed".
It's no good being chicken-hearted.
We die; that's that; our flesh decays
Or disappears in other ways.
But since we're Christians, we believe
That we new bodies will receive
To clothe our souls for us to meet
Our Maker at his Judgement Seat.
And this belief's a gift of faith

And, if it's true, no end is death.
Mid-Lent is passed and Easter's near
The greatest day of all the year
When Jesus, who indeed had died,
Rose with his body glorified.
And if you find believing hard
The primroses in your churchyard
And modern science too will show
That all things change the while they grow,
And we, who change in Time will be
Still more changed in Eternity.

In Memory of George Whitby, Architect

Si monumentum requiris . . . the church in which we are sitting,
Its firm square ceiling supported by fluted Corinthian columns
In groups of three at the corners, its huge semi-circular windows
Lighting the elegant woodwork and plaster panels and gilding:
Look around you, behold the work of Nicholas Hawksmoor.

Si monumentum requiris . . . not far away and behind us
Rises the dome of Saint Paul's, around it a forest of steeples
In Portland stone and in lead, a human and cheerful collection,
Mostly by Christopher Wren, Nicholas Hawksmoor's master.
Si monumentum requiris . . . at the western gate of the City
Behold the Law's new fortress, ramparting over the Bailey
In cream-coloured clear-cut ashlar on grim granitic foundations—
But, like all good citizens, paying regard to its neighbours,
Florid baroque on one side, plain commercial the other.

This is your work, George Whitby, whose name to-day we
                                    remember:
From Donald McMorran and Dance to Wren and Nicholas
                                    Hawksmoor,
You stand in a long tradition; and we who are left salute you.

[Delivered at Saint Mary Woolnoth, 29 March 1973.]

WHEATFIELD, OXON

Septuagesima

Septuagesima—seventy days
To Easter's primrose tide of praise;
The Gesimas—Septua, Sexa, Quinc
Mean Lent is near, which makes you think.
Septuagesima—when we're told
To "run the race", to "keep our hold",
Ignore injustice, not give in,
And practise stern self-discipline;
A somewhat unattractive time
Which hardly lends itself to rhyme.

    But still it gives the chance to me
To praise our dear old C. of E.
So other Churches please forgive

Lines on the Church in which I live,
The Church of England of my birth,
The kindest Church to me on earth.
There may be those who like things fully
Argued out, and call you "woolly";
Ignoring Creeds and Catechism
They say the C. of E.'s "in schism".
There may be those who much resent
Priest, Liturgy, and Sacrament,
Whose worship is what they call "free",
Well, let them be so, but for me
There's refuge in the C. of E.
And when it comes that I must die
I hope the Vicar's standing by,
I won't care if he's "Low" or "High"
For he'll be there to aid my soul
On that dread journey to its goal,
With Sacrament and prayer and Blessing
After I've done my last confessing.
And at that time may I receive
The Grace most firmly to believe,
For if the Christian's Faith's untrue
What is the point of me and you?
    But this is all anticipating
Septuagesima—time of waiting,
Running the race or holding fast.
Let's praise the man who goes to light
The church stove on an icy night.
Let's praise that hard-worked he or she
The Treasurer of the P.C.C.
Let's praise the cleaner of the aisles,

The nave and candlesticks and tiles.
Let's praise the organist who tries
To make the choir increase in size,
Or if that simply cannot be,
Just to improve its quality.
Let's praise the ringers in the tower
Who come to ring in cold and shower.
But most of all let's praise the few
Who are seen in their accustomed pew
Throughout the year, whate'er the weather,
That they may worship God together.
These, like a fire of glowing coals,
Strike warmth into each other's souls,
And though they be but two or three
They keep the Church for you and me.

Perp. Revival i' the North

O, I wad gang tae Harrogate
  Tae a kirk by Temple Moore,
Wi' a tall choir and a lang nave
  And rush mats on the floor;
And Percy Dearmer chasubles
  And nae pews but chairs,
And there we'll sing the Sarum rite
  Tae English Hymnal airs.

It's a far cry frae Harrogate
  And mony a heathery mile
Tae a stane kirk wi' a wee spire
  And a verra wee south aisle.
The rhododendrons bloom wi'oot
  On ilka Simmer's day,
And it's there the Airl o' Feversham
  Wad hae his tenants pray;
For there's something in the painted roof
  And the mouldings round the door,
The braw bench and the plain font
  That tell's o' Temple Moore.

Our Padre

Our padre is an old sky pilot,
  Severely now they've clipped his wings,
But still the flagstaff in the Rect'ry garden
  Points to Higher Things.

Still he has got a hearty handshake;
  Still he wears his medals and a stole;
His voice would reach to Heaven, *and* make
  The Rock of Ages Roll.

He's too sincere to join the high church
  Worshipping idols for the Lord,
And, though the lowest church is my church,
  Our padre's Broad.

Our padre is an old sky pilot,
  He's tied a reef knot round my heart,
We'll be rocked up to Heaven on a rare old tune—
  Come on—take part!

CHORUS

  (*Sung*) Pull for the shore, sailor, pull for the shore!
      Heed not the raging billow, bend to the oar!
    Bend to the oar before the padre!
      Proud, with the padre rowing stroke!
    Good old padre! God for the services!
      Row like smoke!

Blame the Vicar

When things go wrong it's rather tame
To find we are ourselves to blame,
It gets the trouble over quicker
To go and blame things on the Vicar.
The Vicar, after all, is paid
To keep us bright and undismayed.
The Vicar is more virtuous too
Than lay folks such as me and you.
He never swears, he never drinks,
He never *should* say what he thinks.
His collar is the wrong way round,
And that is why he's simply bound
To be the sort of person who
Has nothing very much to do
But take the blame for what goes wrong
And sing in tune at Evensong.

For what's a Vicar really for
Except to cheer us up? What's more,
He shouldn't ever, ever tell
If there is such a place as Hell,
For if there is it's certain he
Will go to it as well as we.
The Vicar should be all pretence
And never, never give offence.
To preach on Sunday is his task
And lend his mower when we ask
And organize our village fêtes
And sing at Christmas with the waits
And in his car to give us lifts

And when we quarrel, heal the rifts.
To keep his family alive
He should industriously strive
In that enormous house he gets,
And he should always pay his debts,
For he has quite six pounds a week,
And when we're rude he should be meek
And always turn the other cheek.
He should be neat and nicely dressed
With polished shoes and trousers pressed,
For we look up to him as higher
Than anyone, except the Squire.

Dear People, who have read so far,
I know how really kind you are,
I hope that you are always seeing
Your Vicar as a human being,
Making allowances when he
Does things with which you don't agree.
But there are lots of people who
Are not so kind to him as you.
So in conclusion you shall hear
About a parish somewhat near,
Perhaps your own or maybe not,
And of the Vicars that it got.
One parson came and people said,
"Alas! Our former Vicar's dead!
And this new man is far more 'Low'
Than dear old Reverend so-and-so,
And far too earnest in his preaching,
We do not really like his teaching,

He seems to think we're simply fools
Who've never been to Sunday Schools."
That Vicar left, and by and by
A new one came, "He's much too 'High',"
The people said, "too like a saint,
His incense makes our Mavis faint."
So now he's left and they're alone
Without a Vicar of their own.
The living's been amalgamated
With one next door they've always hated.

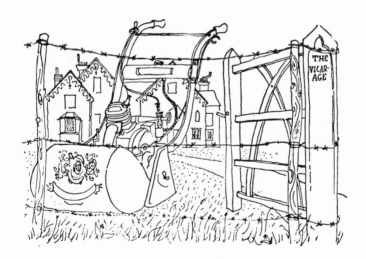